Maggie Adopts a Kitten

(It really happened!)

A woof and a meow
to you!

Marci Kladnik

MAGGIE

Barney

Look for these Maggies stories by Marci Kladnik coming soon. They really happened!

Maggie and Barney and the Allergic Photographer

Maggie and the Long Shadows

Maggie and the Magic Window Seat

Maggie Gets Into Trouble

Maggies' Special Animal Friends

Maggie and the Smelly Stuff

Maggie Adopts a Kitten

(It really happened!)

Marci Kladnik

Illustrated by Stephanie Piro

Maggie Adopts a Kitten (It really happened!)

ISBN: 978-1-7345516-0-0 (hardcover)
ISBN: 978-1-7345516-1-7 (paperback)

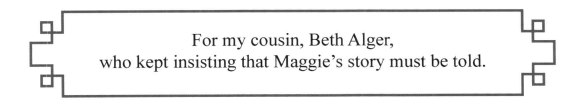

For my cousin, Beth Alger,
who kept insisting that Maggie's story must be told.

Maggie was a Scottish terrier. From the very beginning, she was different. It wasn't because her right ear didn't stand up the way a Scottie's ears are supposed to. It wasn't because she liked raw carrots while her littermates spit them out. It was because she liked cats.

Her mother and father disliked cats, and so did all her brothers and sisters. Any cat that dared come into their backyard was promptly chased over the fence and barked at quite loudly. Only new cats in the neighborhood ever made the mistake of going into that yard. No cat EVER went back.

Maggie never joined in the chase but would sit quietly and watch from a safe distance.

One day when Maggie was old enough to leave her mother and father, she went to live with a nice lady named Marci. It was a long way from home, and the puppy was scared. She was so frightened during the car trip that she peed in her crate and arrived somewhat soggy.

Marci didn't care. She held her new puppy close, scratched her head, and let Maggie lick her face. Maggie felt much better after that.

Maggie's old backyard had been mostly dirt, so when Marci set the puppy down on grass, the little dog was very happy.

Maggie ran down the long backyard, circled around a pink and white gazebo, then ran back the other way and circled around the stone fire pit. She had her own racetrack and loved it! She ran and ran until she collapsed, panting at Marci's feet.

After a rest and a drink of cool, fresh water, Marci took the puppy inside to meet... THE CATS!

Now remember, Maggie had never met a cat face-to-face. She had only seen them streaking by when her brothers and sisters had chased them over the fence. Maggie's eyes opened wide with excitement when she saw a large orange cat sleeping in a patch of sunlight on the floor.

She trotted over for a curious sniff.

The cat's name was Punkin. He didn't run away because he knew that Maggie was just a puppy. Their wet noses rubbed together in greeting. The cat yawned, curled up, and went back to sleep.

Just then a shiny black cat named Dodo came out to see what was going on. The cat's yellow eyes narrowed when he saw the dog.

Dodo was Punkin's brother, but they were very different as siblings sometimes are. Punkin was orange and Dodo was black. Dodo liked avocado (which is not good for cats!) and Punkin preferred tuna. Most of all, Punkin liked dogs and Dodo did not—even if they were just puppies.

Maggie didn't know this as she trotted up to the black cat, ready to make another new friend.

That's when Maggie learned about CLAWS!

Quick as lightning, Dodo's paw shot out and scratched the puppy's tender nose!

Poor little Maggie squealed and ran behind Marci to hide.

Marci picked the frightened puppy up to comfort her as the black cat stalked off with his tail proudly held high.

Maggie was not really hurt. She was just so surprised that Dodo didn't want to make friends.

Every day Maggie would try again to make friends with Dodo, but she was always very careful to keep her nose out of reach of those sharp claws.

It took a long time before Dodo stopped hissing at Maggie. Eventually Dodo accepted Maggie and then they would eat right next to each other.

A few months after coming to live with Marci and the cats, Maggie was taken to the veterinarian for an operation called spaying. It meant that Maggie would never have any puppies of her own. Marci was a little sad about that, but she knew that it would help keep Maggie healthy.

Maggie healed quickly and soon returned to her upstairs window seat where she liked to watch the comings and goings in the neighborhood all day long. She was a good watchdog and always barked loudly when a strange cat, car, or person came into view. She barked especially loud if someone came into the yard. Punkin and Dodo would always run and hide when Maggie barked like that. Maggie was very good at her job.

Marci had an important job too besides caring for Maggie, Dodo, and Punkin. She took care of feral cats that lived on the streets and under bushes. They were often hungry and sick, and needed help. Sometimes Marci caught little kittens and found them loving homes.

One summer evening, Marci was trying to catch a small kitten that had been all alone for a whole day and night. His mother, brothers, and sisters had been rescued and were all playing together in a foster home. Marci wanted to catch this kitten so she could reunite the family.

The tiny kitten peeked down at her from the dusty rafters of an old dark shed. It was a sweet little gray and white face that could be clearly seen through the dim light and cobwebs, even though he was trying to hide as his mother had taught him to do whenever she left her kittens alone.

Marci knew the kitten had to be hungry. She put some tasty cat food into a trap and meowed softly. She tiptoed quietly out of the building and stood by a dirty window, watching and waiting silently.

It took a long time before the terrified kitten decided his growling tummy was more important than staying hidden. He was, after all, VERY hungry! He climbed down carefully, following his nose toward the delicious smell.

When the kitten went into the trap to eat, the door suddenly closed behind him. He was very scared, and hissed at Marci as she approached, but he was caught. To calm him, Marci covered the trap with a sheet before carrying it to her car.

It was too late to take the kitten to join his family, so Marci took him home with her for the night. She parked her car in the garage and closed the big door. It was dark and quiet and safe for the frightened kitten caught in a cage.

Growing kittens need to eat often, and Marci knew this. She brought food, water, and a small litter box to put into the cage, but the kitten spit and slashed with his claws as she came close! Marci spilled the water all over her clothes as she jumped back in surprise.

Calming herself, she approached the cage again very carefully, and managed to slip the litter box and dishes inside without letting the kitten escape. All the while, the kitten hissed and spit and slashed with his claws. He was very fierce because he was very scared. Marci would be very glad to take this kitten to join his brothers and sisters!

In the morning Marci went to check on him and take the little one some breakfast. She carefully lifted the sheet that covered the trap and peeked in. The kitten was backed into the corner of his cage, trembling and mewing. But when he saw Marci, he rushed spitting and slashing with his sharp claws just as he had done the night before.

Marci was heartbroken to see how terrified the kitten was. She wanted to pick him up and cuddle him, but she was afraid to get near the cage.

"Perhaps if he saw I LIKE cats...," she thought, and went inside to get her black kitty.

The kitten's mother was black, so Marci hoped that seeing Dodo in her arms would calm the kitten down. She held Dodo up a safe distance away from the cage.

Dodo hissed and struggled to get down.

Then Marci tried it again with Punkin.

Neither Punkin nor Dodo wanted anything to do with the kitten.

The poor little kitten continued to shake and cry and hiss and spit.

Then Marci thought of Maggie. She was black too and liked cats.

When Marci picked Maggie up to see the kitten, a miraculous thing happened.

THE KITTEN STOPPED SHAKING AND HE STARTED PURRING VERY LOUDLY!

He slowly came forward towards Maggie. Then he reached out to the dog through the cage with his tiny paw, still purring loudly.

Marci brought Maggie a bit closer.

The kitten purred.

The kitten and dog touched noses.

The kitten purred.

Maggie sniffed the kitten.

The kitten purred.

Still afraid of those sharp claws, Marci slowly reached out a finger and stroked the soft fur through the cage bars.

The kitten purred.

Obviously it was LOVE at first sight between Maggie and the kitten!

Maggie wiggled excitedly in Marci's arms.

Marci carefully opened the cage and lifted the kitten out. She gently placed him on her lap and watched in amazement as Maggie nuzzled his tiny face and licked him. The kitten just purred and purred, rubbing against Maggie.

Marci took the pair into the house and put them together in a room without Punkin or Dodo. The kitten never left the dog's side, and Maggie couldn't have been happier as she sniffed and licked her new baby. The only time she moved away was when the kitten would try to nurse because, you see, Maggie didn't have any milk to give him.

By now Marci realized a very special bond had formed between Maggie and the kitten. Although she hadn't planned on adopting another cat, she knew that this kitten would be joining the family.

Now he needed a name. Since Marci caught the kitten in a small barn-like shed, she decided to name the kitten Barney.

Barney spent all his time with Maggie. They chased each other up and down the hallway upstairs. Afterwards they napped together on the window seat overlooking the neighborhood.

When Marci took Maggie out for their daily walk, Barney would watch from the window until "Mommy Maggie" returned.

Little Barney wouldn't even eat unless Maggie was there beside him. Maggie loved cat food (even though it was too rich for her), and would lick Barney's face after every meal.

Cats like to play at night, so they need to be taught when to sleep if they are going to live in a house with people. At bedtime, Marci put Barney into a bathroom by himself. She did this to keep him safe and so he would learn to sleep when she did.

One night Marci went to bed and didn't lock Barney into his room. She was just falling asleep when loud purring woke her up. It wasn't coming from Punkin who was at her feet. It wasn't coming from Dodo who was on her pillow. Oddly the sound was coming from the bed on the floor where Maggie slept!

Marci looked over the side of her bed, and there was Barney all snuggled up next to his mom. Maggie's big head and Barney's tiny one were side-by-side hanging over the edge of the pillow.

Marci just smiled, turned over and went to sleep. She knew Barney was in the good paws of his "Mommy Maggie." Marci was very glad that Maggie had a baby after all, even if it was a kitten!

It really happened!

Marci with Maggie as a puppy in front of the pink and white house that matched the gazebo

Dodo

Punkin

Maggie and Barney on the window seat

Barney and Maggie that first night in bed

Maggie with her floppy right ear

Lesson:

Girl cats and dogs should be spayed and boy cats and dogs should be neutered because it helps them be healthier and to live longer. It also improves their behavior around other animals and people.

The most important reason to spay and neuter dogs and cats is to prevent the birth of unwanted puppies and kittens. There are not enough homes for all the puppies and kittens in the world.

Many cats born on the street like Barney are called feral because they don't have a home. If no one like Marci takes care of the kittens born outside, they are hungry and often get sick. They may even die. Even kittens born in homes are not always wanted and the people put them out on the street or take them to places called animal shelters where they are put into cages.

Visit a local animal shelter and see for yourself all the cats and dogs living in small cages instead of in loving homes. Maybe your family could adopt one or two of them.

Quiz:

1. What is a feral cat?

   a. A cat or kitten that lives in a house with people.

   b. A cat or kitten that lives on the street and under bushes.

   c. An injured or sick cat or kitten.

2. Why should cats and dogs be spayed and neutered?

   a. It prevents the birth of unwanted puppies and kittens.

   b. It is healthier for the pets so they live longer.

   c. Both of the above.

3. What happens to cats that are born on the street if no one takes care of them?

   a. They are often hungry and sick.

   b. They live happily in the bushes and have lots of kitty friends to play with.

   c. They get lots of fleas that make them itch.

4. What happens at an animal shelter?

   a. Cats and dogs are kept in small cages.

   b. People can find cats and dogs to adopt.

   c. Both of the above.

Answers: b, c, a, c

Marci Kladnik is an award-winning writer and photographer. She has won multiple MUSE medallions and Certificates of Excellence from the Cat Writers' Association and was a finalist for a Maxwell from the Dog Writers Association of America. For seven years she wrote a newspaper column about feral cats while sitting on the board of Catalyst for Cats, Inc. Her work has been published in books and magazines and she continues to write for various online and print publications. Marci served as president of the Cat Writers' Association for four years. She lives in the tiny town of Los Alamos, CA with her dog and three cats.

Visit her website: www.maggiestories.com

Stephanie Piro is an award-winning cartoonist, illustrator and designer. She is one of King Features' team of women cartoonists, "Six Chix", now in its 20th year of syndication. She has won multiple MUSE medallions and Certificates of Excellence from the Cat Writers' Association and has been nominated for the National Cartoonists' Society's Reuben Award in the Single Panel Newspaper division for her single panel "Far Game". Stephanie lives in New Hampshire with her husband and three cats.

Visit her website: www.stephaniepiro.com

CPSIA information can be obtained at www.ICGtesting.com
Printed in the USA
LVIW012119170920
666234LV00002B/18